Bill Gillian
'80

ELEPHANT FACTS

BY
BOB BARNER

A Unicorn Book   E. P. Dutton   New York

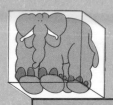

Library of Congress Cataloging in Publication Data
Barner, Bob.   Elephant facts.
(A Unicorn book)

SUMMARY: Presents numerous facts about the ancestry,
growth, habits, and behavior of the largest
land animal.
1. Elephants—Juvenile literature. [1. Elephants]   I. Title.
QL737.P98B28   599'.61   79-11226   ISBN 0-525-29200-4

Published in the United States by E. P. Dutton, a Division
of Elsevier-Dutton Publishing Company, Inc., New York
Published simultaneously in Canada by Clarke,
Irwin & Company Limited, Toronto and Vancouver

Editor: Emilie McLeod   Designer: Patricia Lowy

Printed in the U.S.A.   First Edition
10 9 8 7 6 5 4 3 2 1

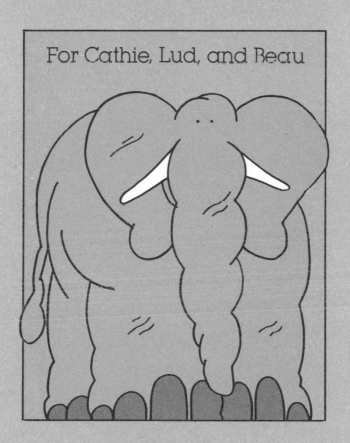

For Cathie, Lud, and Beau

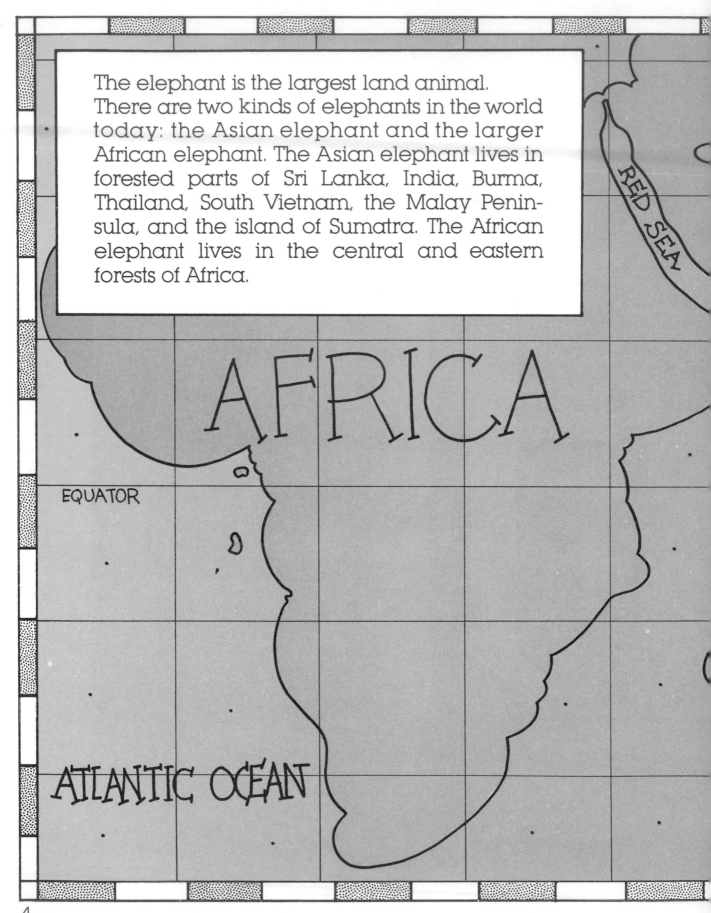

The elephant is the largest land animal. There are two kinds of elephants in the world today: the Asian elephant and the larger African elephant. The Asian elephant lives in forested parts of Sri Lanka, India, Burma, Thailand, South Vietnam, the Malay Peninsula, and the island of Sumatra. The African elephant lives in the central and eastern forests of Africa.

AFRICA

RED SEA

EQUATOR

ATLANTIC OCEAN

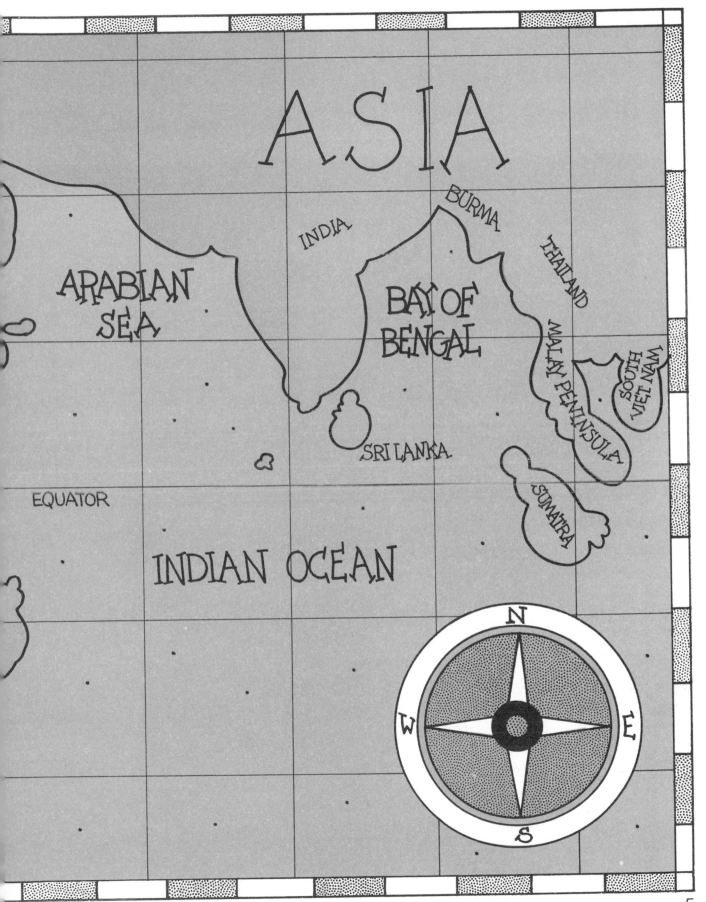

ASIA

BURMA

INDIA

THAILAND

ARABIAN
SEA

BAY OF
BENGAL

MALAY PENINSULA

SOUTH
VIET NAM

SRI LANKA

SUMATRA

EQUATOR

INDIAN OCEAN

N

W   E

S

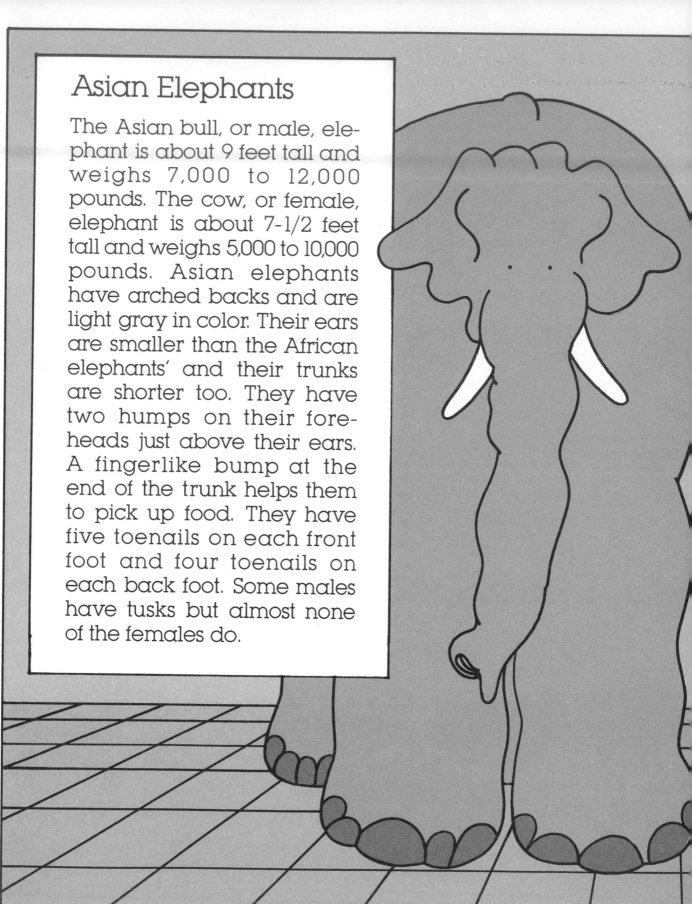

Asian Elephants

The Asian bull, or male, elephant is about 9 feet tall and weighs 7,000 to 12,000 pounds. The cow, or female, elephant is about 7-1/2 feet tall and weighs 5,000 to 10,000 pounds. Asian elephants have arched backs and are light gray in color. Their ears are smaller than the African elephants' and their trunks are shorter too. They have two humps on their foreheads just above their ears. A fingerlike bump at the end of the trunk helps them to pick up food. They have five toenails on each front foot and four toenails on each back foot. Some males have tusks but almost none of the females do.

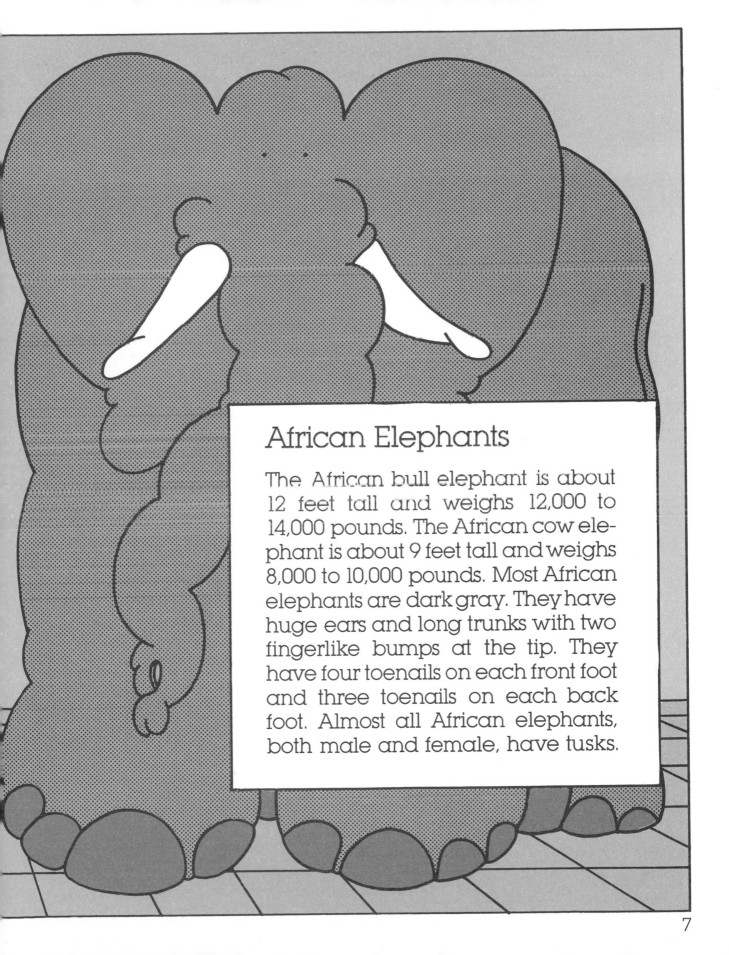

African Elephants

The African bull elephant is about 12 feet tall and weighs 12,000 to 14,000 pounds. The African cow elephant is about 9 feet tall and weighs 8,000 to 10,000 pounds. Most African elephants are dark gray. They have huge ears and long trunks with two fingerlike bumps at the tip. They have four toenails on each front foot and three toenails on each back foot. Almost all African elephants, both male and female, have tusks.

The Wooly Mammoth

Elephants are descended from the wooly mammoths who lived before the Ice Age in North America, Europe, and Asia. The mammoth was about 13 feet tall and 15 feet long with 8-foot tusks and thick, wooly hair 12 inches long. The mammoths died out gradually as the climate cooled and food became scarce. They were hunted by cavemen for their meat and warm skins. The frozen body of a mammoth was found in Russia in 1846. The beast's hair, skin, tusks, and insides were in perfect condition.

ELEPHANT TRIVIA

JUMBO WAS THE WORLD'S MOST FAMOUS ELEPHANT.

HE PERFORMED IN P.T. BARNUM'S CIRCUS FROM 1882 TO 1885.

ONE MILLION CHILDREN RODE ON JUMBO'S BACK.

The skull is very strong to support the large tusks, but is light for its size, so the elephant can move its head easily.

Elephants can't see as well as people do.

An elephant can hold 2 gallons of water in its trunk.

Elephants have only four teeth. Each tooth is 1 foot long and weighs 9 pounds.

Blood is cooled as it passes through the ears.

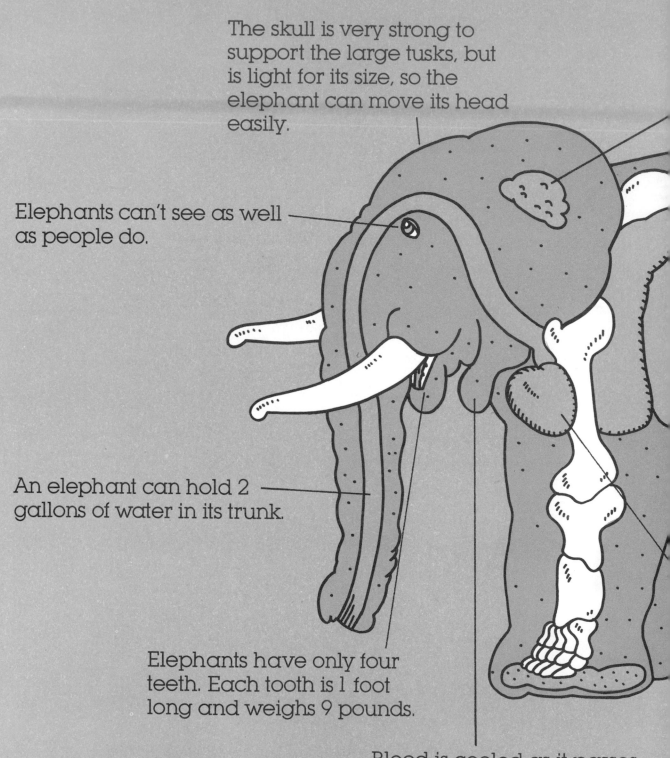

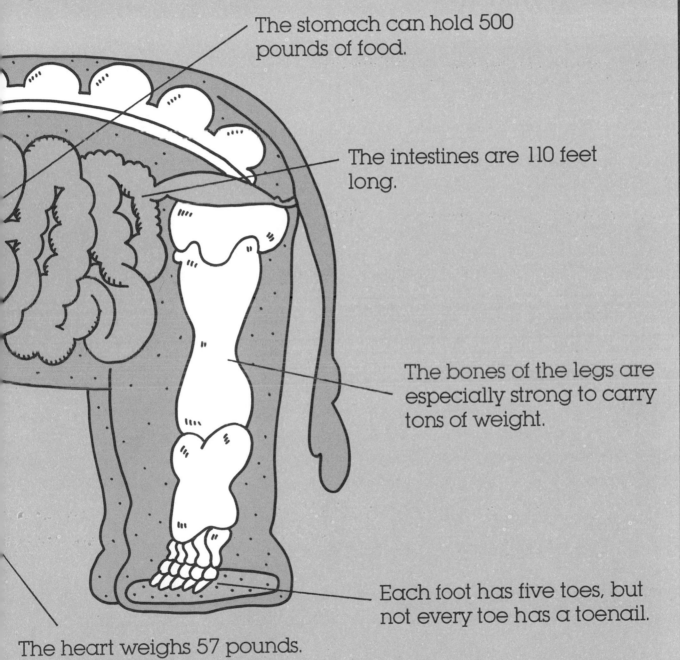

The elephant's brain weighs 11 pounds. Our brain weighs 3 pounds.

The stomach can hold 500 pounds of food.

The intestines are 110 feet long.

The bones of the legs are especially strong to carry tons of weight.

Each foot has five toes, but not every toe has a toenail.

The heart weighs 57 pounds. It beats 35 times per minute. Human hearts beat 70 times in a minute.

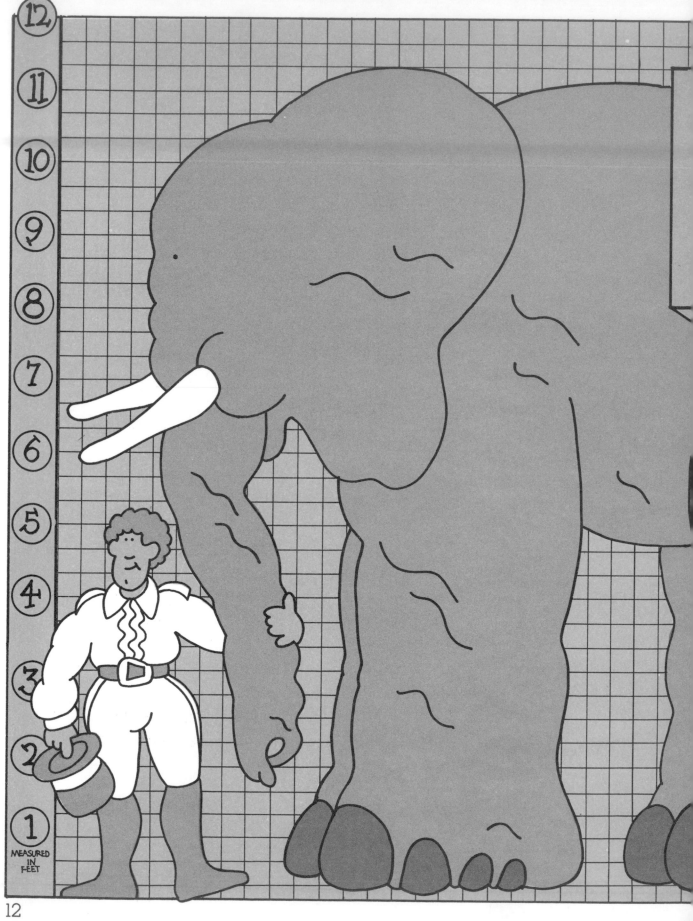

12

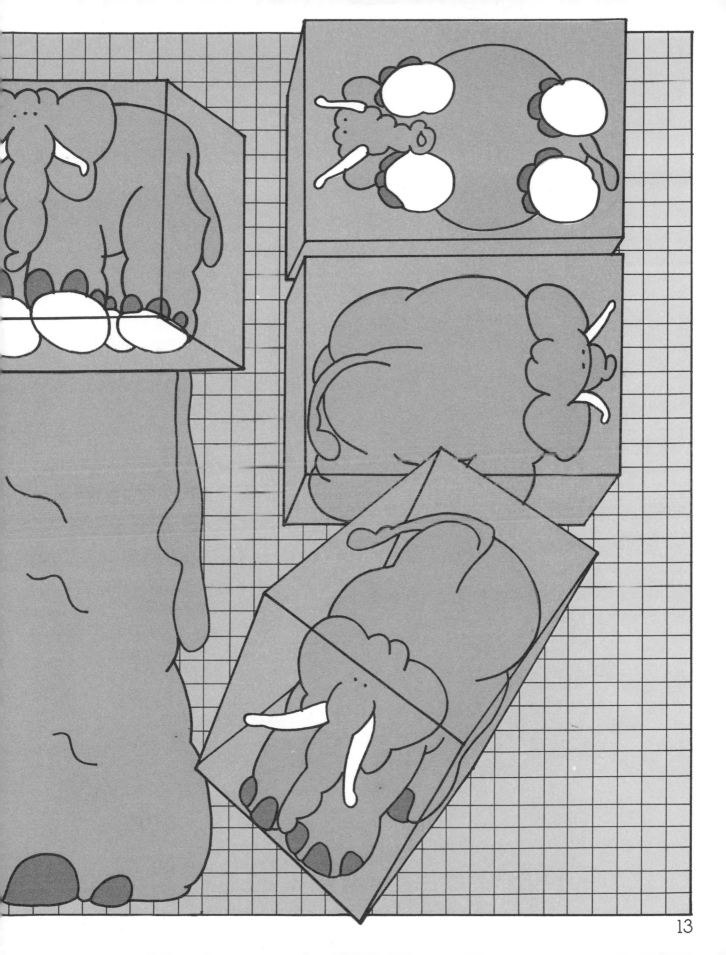

13

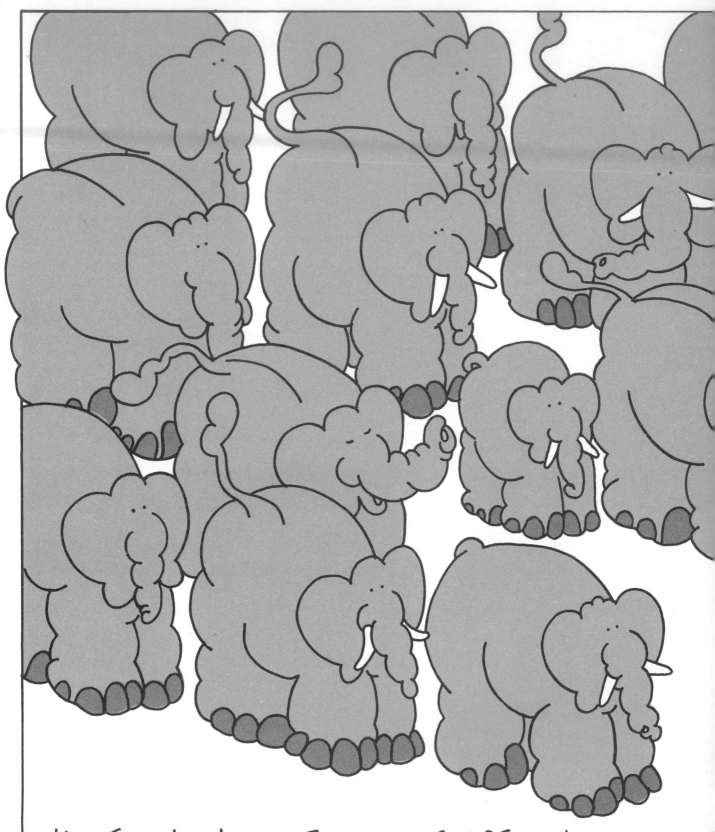

Elephants travel in single file at a speed

Wild elephants live in herds of ten to fifty or more. The leader of the herd is usually an older female.

of about 6 miles an hour.

The elephant's skin is 1½ inches thick and weighs 2,000 pounds.

One elephant hair is as thick as a pencil lead. It can be used to make jewelry, especially rings.

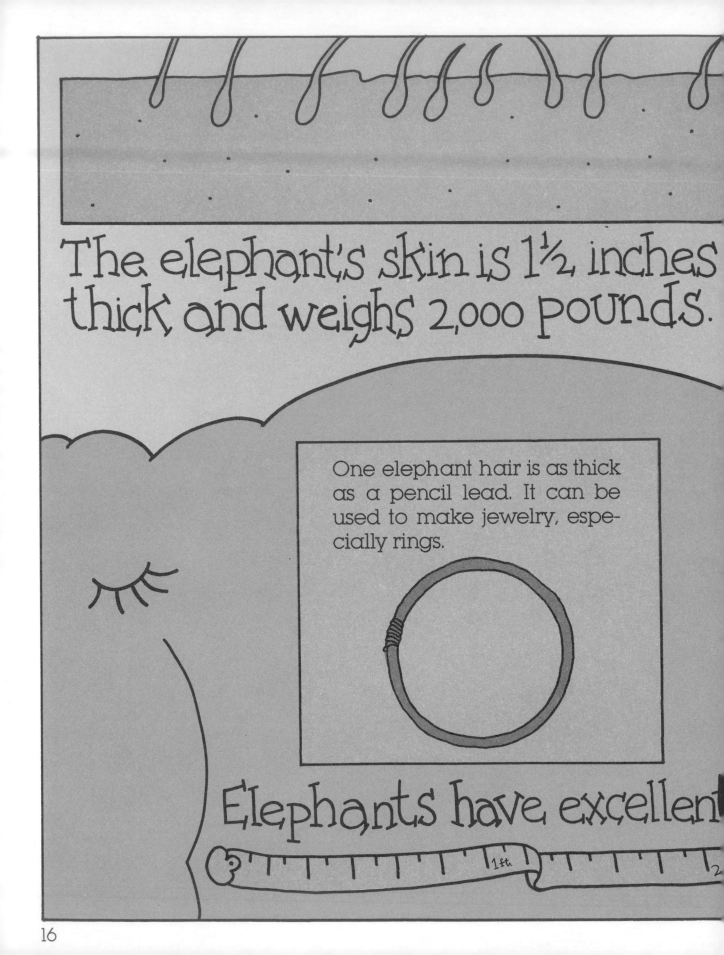

Elephants have excellent

1 ft.

A few elephants are white or albino. Pygmy elephants are only 7 feet tall and weigh 2,000 pounds.

hearing. Some have ears 4 feet wide.

Elephants can swim under water with only the tips of their trunks in the air. They can swim for six hours without stopping.

Noisy Elephants

Elephants move through the forests and plains very quietly if they sense any danger. But, when they feel safe, they can be the noisiest animals in the world. They crack branches off trees and spray water. They chirp, squeal, and make trumpet noises through their trunks. Their stomachs rumble like thunder when they eat.

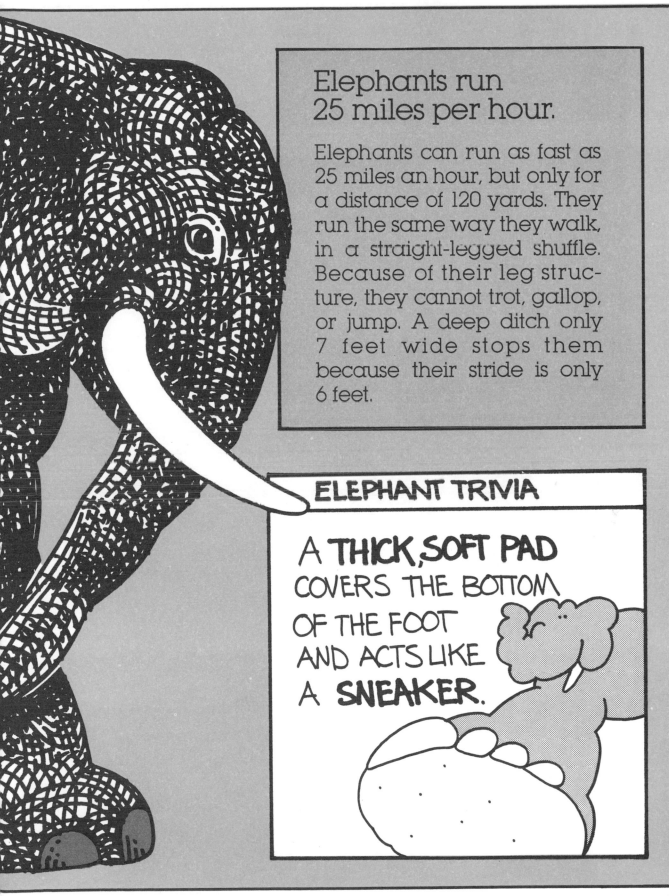

Elephants run 25 miles per hour.

Elephants can run as fast as 25 miles an hour, but only for a distance of 120 yards. They run the same way they walk, in a straight-legged shuffle. Because of their leg structure, they cannot trot, gallop, or jump. A deep ditch only 7 feet wide stops them because their stride is only 6 feet.

ELEPHANT TRIVIA

A **THICK, SOFT PAD** COVERS THE BOTTOM OF THE FOOT AND ACTS LIKE A **SNEAKER**.

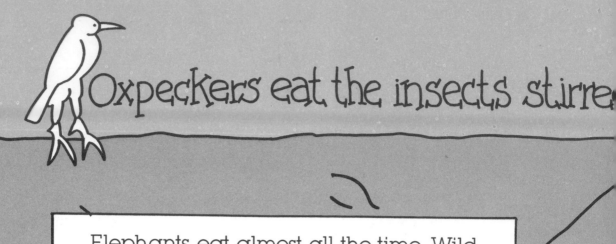

Elephants eat almost all the time. Wild elephants eat up to 500 pounds of bark, leaves, and grass each day. Tame elephants eat about 300 pounds of hay, carrots, apples and bread each day.

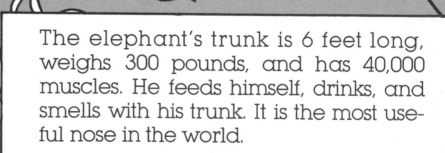

The elephant's trunk is 6 feet long, weighs 300 pounds, and has 40,000 muscles. He feeds himself, drinks, and smells with his trunk. It is the most useful nose in the world.

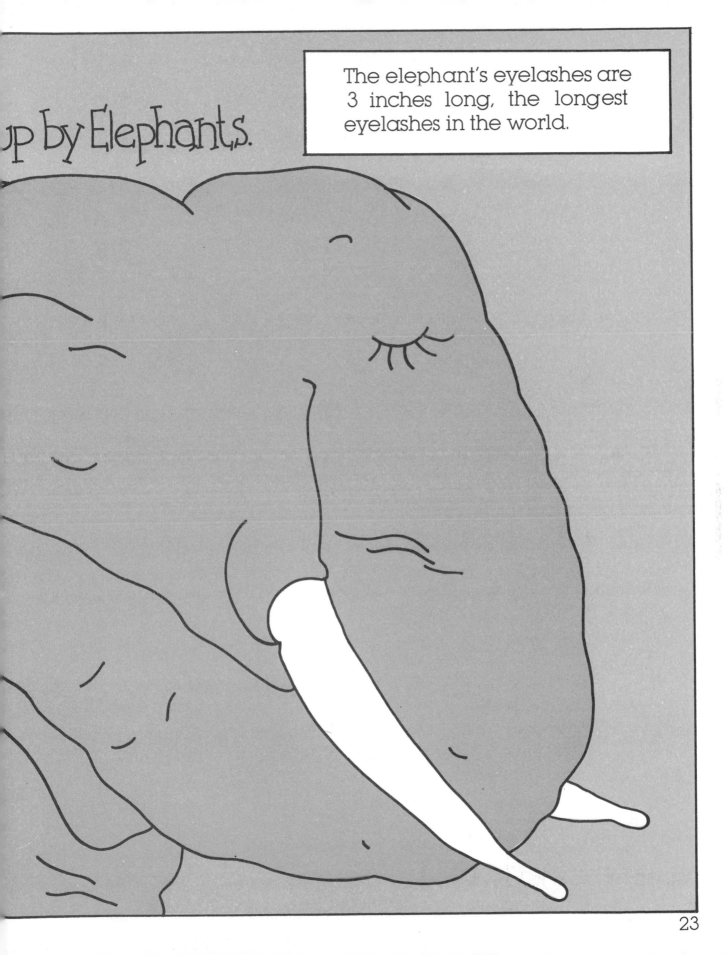

up by Elephants.

The elephant's eyelashes are 3 inches long, the longest eyelashes in the world.

Tusks are long solid teeth used to slash at trees and dig up roots for food. When two male elephants fight, they use their tusks as weapons. Two fighting females will try to bite off each other's tail.

Some elephant tusks are 11 feet.

Elephant tusks are pure ivory. They were used to make piano keys.

Elephant tusks are solid ivory. They were used to make piano keys. People have been carving jewelry and figures from ivory for more than 20,000 years.

Long and weigh 300 pounds.

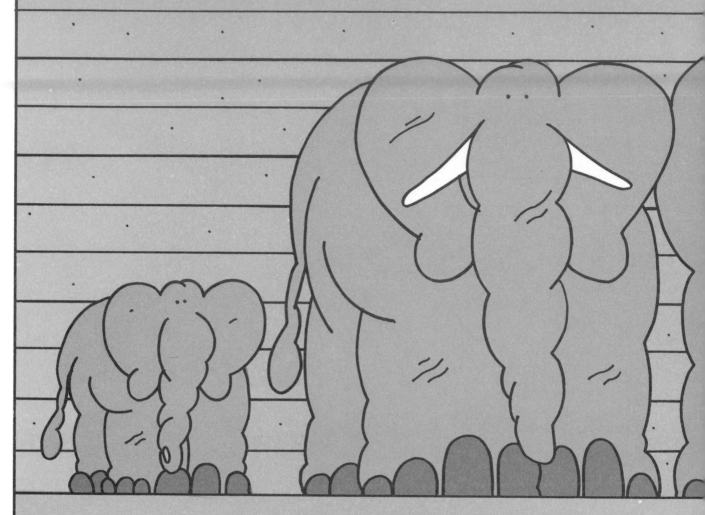

Calf

Age: Birth to 5 years
The calf weighs about 200 pounds and is about 3 feet tall at birth. Baby calves stay very close to their mothers for food and protection. They learn to find food, follow the herd, and play.

Young Adult

Age: 5 to 15 years
The young adult weighs about 5,000 pounds and is about 6 feet tall. Young elephants like to play and swim. They learn the ways of the herd during these years.

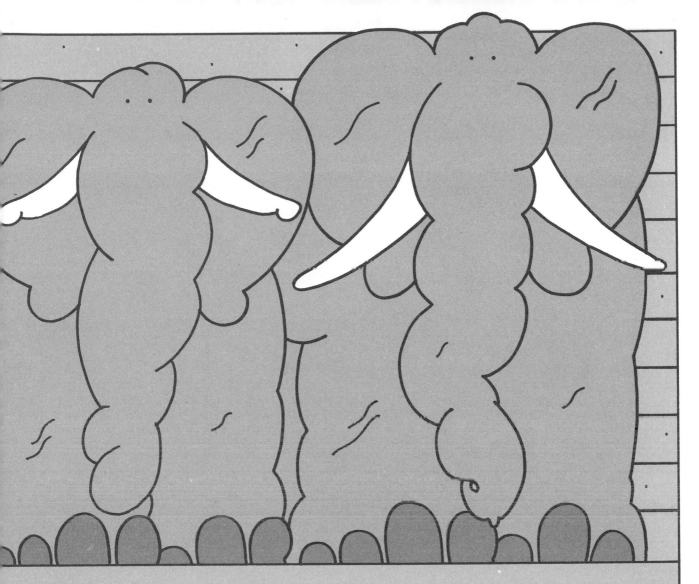

Adult

Age: 15 to 50 years
The adult weighs about 10,000 pounds and is 10 feet tall. When elephants are 12 to 15 years old, they are ready to mate. Courtship begins between young males and females. The males may fight other young bulls who want to court the same cow.

Old Adult

Age: Over 50 years
When the adults slow and age, they are cared for and protected by younger members of the family. Some dangerous old elephants, called rogues, attack people and animals. Rogues are bulls suffering pain from decayed teeth, wounds, or a disease.

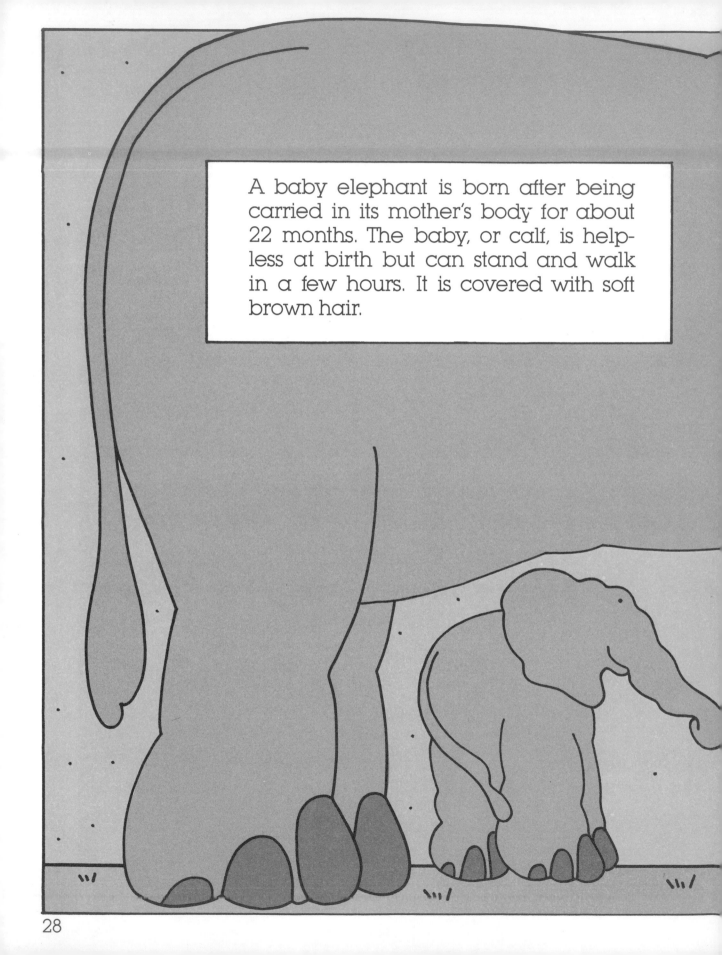

A baby elephant is born after being carried in its mother's body for about 22 months. The baby, or calf, is helpless at birth but can stand and walk in a few hours. It is covered with soft brown hair.

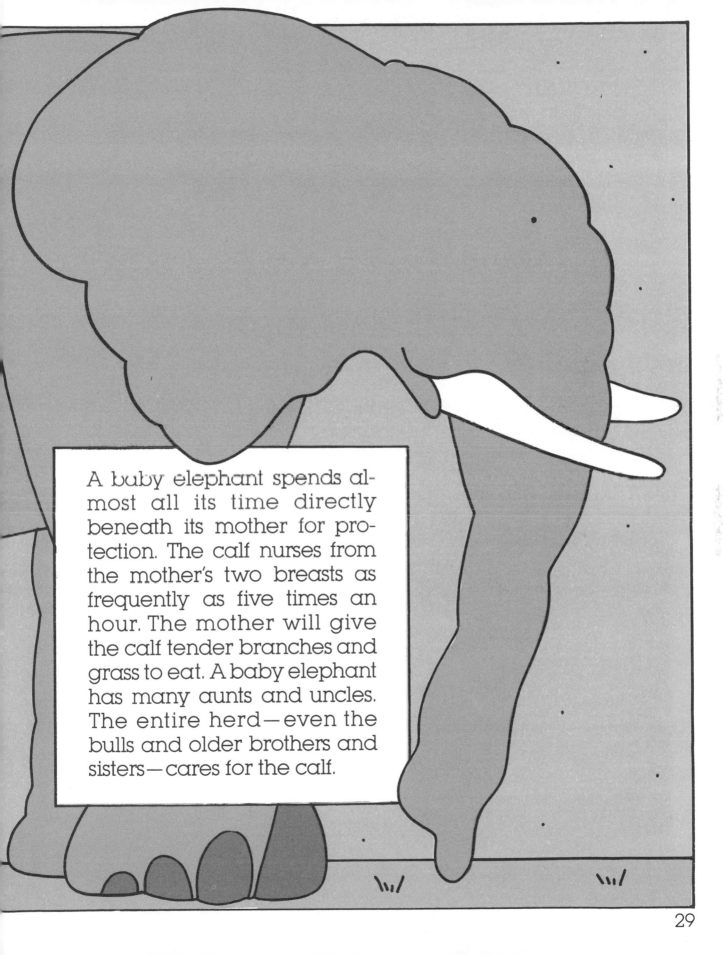

A baby elephant spends almost all its time directly beneath its mother for protection. The calf nurses from the mother's two breasts as frequently as five times an hour. The mother will give the calf tender branches and grass to eat. A baby elephant has many aunts and uncles. The entire herd—even the bulls and older brothers and sisters—cares for the calf.

AN ELEPHANT'S DAY

ELEPHANTS LIKE TO BATHE EVERY DAY.
THEY SHOWER TO COOL THEMSELVES.

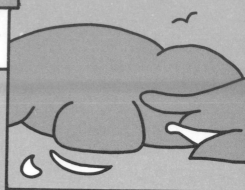

AFTER A SHOWER,
IN THE COOL MUD

THEY HAVE NO HOME, NEED NO SHELTER.

TO KEEP
ELEPHANTS
OF TREES.

ALL THE MEMBERS OF THE HERD TRAVEL TOGETHER IN
THE HUNT FOR FOOD. THEY MOVE VERY QUIETLY AND
SLOWLY SO THE VERY YOUNG AND OLD CAN KEEP PACE.

WHEN THE MUD HAS DRIED, THE ELEPHANTS SCRATCH THEMSELVES AGAINST A ROCK OR TREE TO REMOVE PARASITES.

5.

...EY REST AND WALLOW ...F THE WATERING HOLE.

...OOL DURING THE DAY, ...UDDLE IN THE SHADE

6.

SOMETIMES THEY SLEEP WHILE THEY ARE STANDING IN THE COOL SHADE.

THEY ARE MOST ACTIVE AT NIGHT. THEN THEY DO MOST OF THEIR TRAVELING AND EATING.

8.

How to Catch an Elephant

The most common way to catch Asian elephants is to drive them into a stockade called a keddah. Men called beaters make as much noise as they can and drive the frightened elephants into the stockade.

Sometimes a tame elephant is used as a decoy to catch a single Asian elephant. When a wild elephant comes to help the tame elephant, it is roped and tied.

Elephants are trapped in both Asia and Africa. A deep pit is dug and covered with branches and dirt. After an elephant falls into the pit, hunters tie the elephant with ropes so it cannot escape. The hunters throw in logs and dirt to raise the level of the pit. Then they lead it out of the shallow pit.

Elephants at work

Push with head.

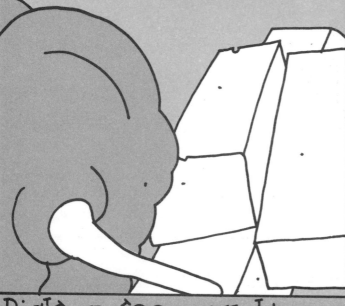

Pull in harness.

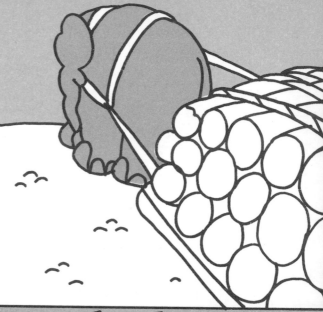

Pick up 600 pounds with trunk.

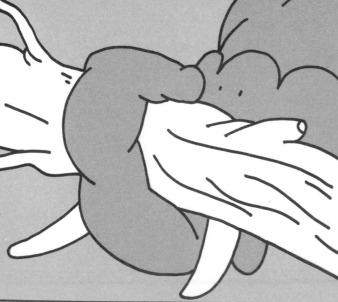

Drag loads with cable in mouth.

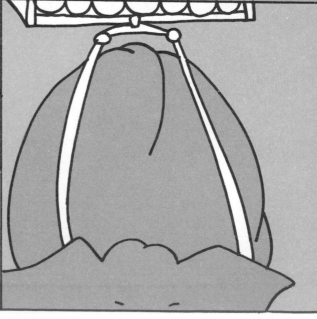

What to take on a safari

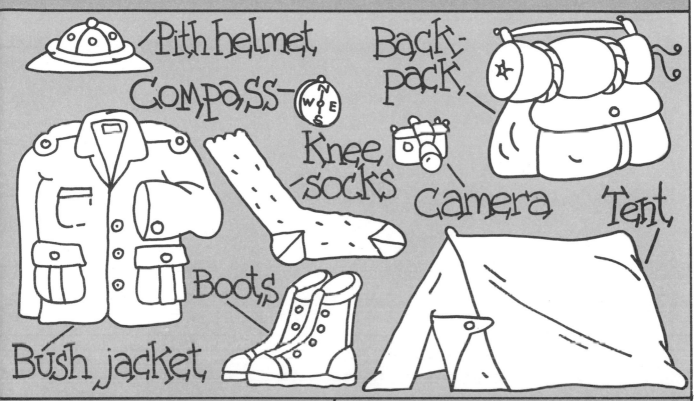

Pith helmet
Compass
Back-pack
Knee-socks
Camera
Tent
Boots
Bush jacket

Dig with tusks.

Carry heavy load.

Circus Elephants

Most circus elephants are female Asian elephants, captured when young. They are gentle and easy to train. If they trust the trainer, they will follow his commands. The most difficult thing to teach an elephant is to ignore loud noises that could scare it while it's performing. Years ago, elephants were used to help put up circus tents and carry heavy equipment. Today, their only job is to perform.

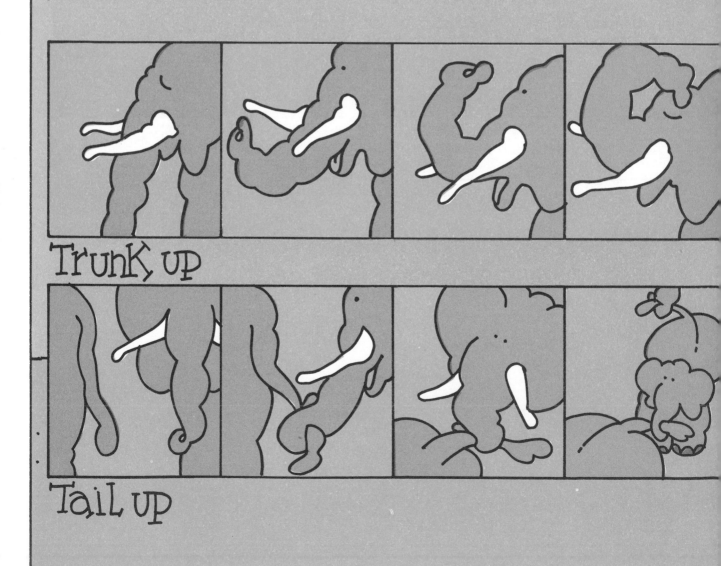

Trunk up

Tail up

A saddle, called a howdah, is used to ride the elephant.

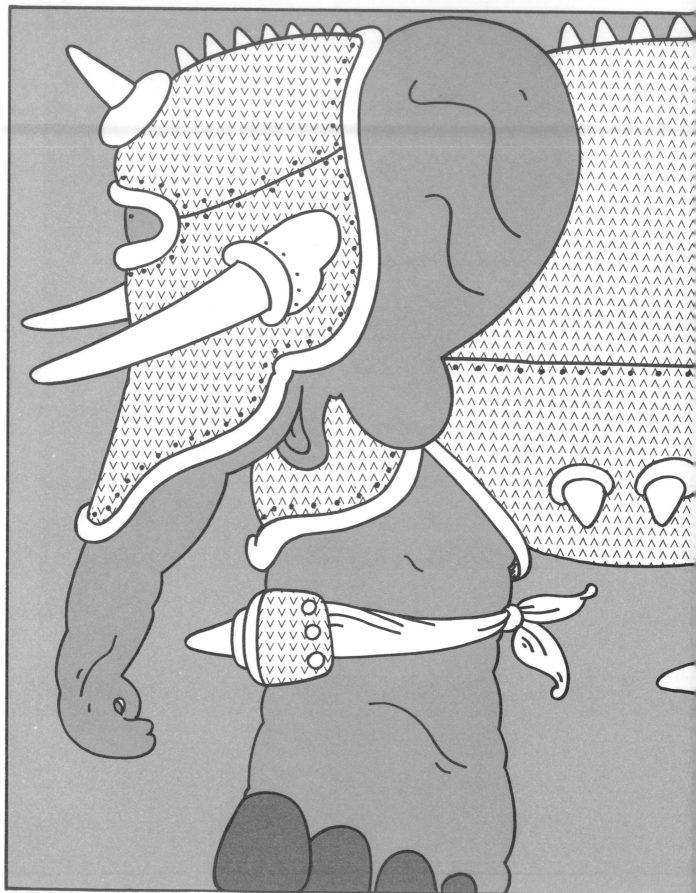

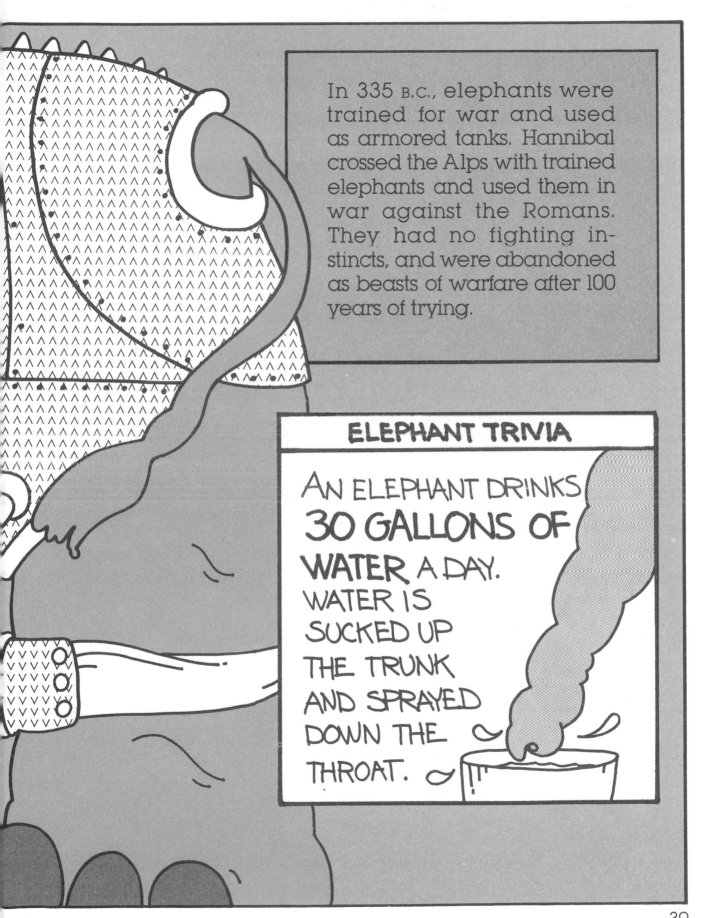

In 335 B.C., elephants were trained for war and used as armored tanks. Hannibal crossed the Alps with trained elephants and used them in war against the Romans. They had no fighting instincts, and were abandoned as beasts of warfare after 100 years of trying.

ELEPHANT TRIVIA

AN ELEPHANT DRINKS **30 GALLONS OF WATER** A DAY. WATER IS SUCKED UP THE TRUNK AND SPRAYED DOWN THE THROAT.

INDEX